ABOUT THE AUTHOR
SIMON CAMBY

Simon is an Educational Consultant working for Focus Education (UK) Ltd. This role involves working with a wide range of primary schools across the UK and overseas. Simon's work involves both training and consultancy. He has worked as a Lead Inspector under the current Ofsted Framework and has also trained new inspectors.

Simon has had experience in the following roles:

- Teacher
- Team Leader
- Deputy Headteacher
- Consultant teacher to school in special measures
- Headteacher
- Senior Advisor for an inner-city Local Education Authority
- Lead Ofsted Inspector.

Simon's main professional interests relate to:

- Leadership development
- Assessment for Learning
- Improving the quality of learning in the classroom
- Curriculum development.

Simon is proactive in his approach to work with schools and ensures that his training and development is based on the most recent research and developments.

Simon has also worked with a wide range of teachers from overseas schools through work at an international summer school held annually in the UK. He took on the role of Co-Director of this summer school in 2005.

First Published in the UK in 2007 by Focus Education (UK) Ltd

Focus Education (UK) Ltd
Talking Point Conference and Exhibition Centre,
Huddersfield Road,
Scouthead,
Oldham,
OL4 4AG

Focus Education (UK) Ltd Reg. No 4507968
ISBN 978-1-904469-58-2

Companies, institutions and other organisations wishing to make bulk purchases books published by Focus Education should contact their local bookstore or Foc Education direct:

Customer Services
Focus Education, Talking Point Conference and Exhibition Centre, Huddersfield Scouthead, Oldham, OL4 4AG   Tel 01457 872427 Fax 01457 878205

INTRODUCTION

INTRODUCTION

Never before has there been a more important time to know about, and understand, the standards and achievement data for your school.

The data in your RAISE on-line report will be the starting point for inspectors when they visit your school. This data, alongside your self-evaluation statement, will help inspectors know the key questions to ask during inspection.

However, it is important to strike a balance. The data should never be seen as the sole domain of inspectors. First and foremost it is for school leaders to use with their staff in order to improve outcomes for children in the school.

Fundamentally, you need to ask the following questions:

This publication is aimed at helping you to answer the first question so that you can confidently make an evaluative statement about the academic outcomes for your school in order to address the second question.

The following sections provide a step-by-step guide of factors to think about and questions to consider when analysing your data. The sections go beyond simple analysis and provide some background information and possible templates for use if you wish to lead training on this area within your own school.

1
Are outcomes good enough, when taking account of the starting points and context of the pupils?

2
What more can we change with provision to improve outcomes for our pupils?

RAISE online stands for…

Reporting and

Analysis for

Improvement through

School

Self **E**valuation

WHAT IS RAISE ON-LINE?

Introduced in 2006, RAISE online is intended to be a single source of information for use by all stakeholders involved in school improvement.

WHO IS IT FOR?

It is intended to be used by:

- Headteachers and their staff
- Inspectors
- DfES, Ofsted and National Strategies
- Local Authorities
- School Improvement Partners

There are also facilities to filter information and generate your own 'personalised' reports looking at issues pertinent to your school context. In addition, schools can enter test data in order to generate question level analysis previously generated by using the Pupil Achievement Tracker (PAT).

WHAT DOES IT CONTAIN?

RAISE online contains all that was outlined in the old PANDA report plus additional information, including:

- attainment information for the end of each key stage
- trends over 5 years for whole school
- attainment information for pupil groups
- attainment information for each core subject
- progress information between key stages 1 and 2
- contextual added value outcomes for progress between key stages 1 and 2 for (i) whole school, (ii) core subjects and (iii) pupil groupings
- interactive reports to 'drill down' from cohort level to individual level

WHAT WILL RAISE ONLINE ENABLE YOU TO DO?

RAISE online should enable you to:

- Examine context, attainment and value added
- Explore hypotheses about pupil performance
- Analyse question level data for national, optional and progress tests
- Analyse performance for a range of centrally predefined and additional school defined pupil groups
- Set and moderate pupil targets

THE **BIG** PICTURE

THE BIG PICTURE BEFORE WE BEGIN

YOUR ANALYSIS NEEDS TO PICK UP ON TWO MAIN ISSUES:

STANDARDS **+** **ACHIEVEMENT**

Many schools are not expressing clear enough judgements about these as separate entities.
This is important if you are to accurately portray what is going on in your school.

Secondly, your evaluation needs to explicitly answer these two BIG questions:

1 Is achievement good enough in your school?

2 Is there any under-achievement in your school?

This publication will help you to answer both of these challenges.

BE CLEAR IN YOUR OWN MIND...

... about the difference between standards and achievement. Ofsted ask schools to be explicit in their evaluation of each in the SEF. Make sure you identify both as distinct factors. Your judgements about each may be the same or may be different.

These words are often used inter-changeably and incorrectly. Many official publications mistake their meaning and this can lead to further confusion. You must ensure that you and your team are absolutely clear about what you mean when you use these words.

ATTAINMENT / STANDARDS	PROGRESS	ACHIEVEMENT
The terms attainment and standards are often used interchangeably to mean the same thing in a school context. Attainment is any measure in relation to nationally agreed levels, *e.g. National Curriculum levels, Early Learning Goals, FSP points, P-scales etc.* Attainment is a 'snapshot in time'. It is important to know about the attainment of individuals, groups and cohorts in your school and setting. Attainment measures in RAISE online as expressed as average point scores and as the percentage of children attaining specific national curriculum levels.	Progress is the distance travelled between two attainment points, *e.g. progress from September to July etc.* Remember that progress is not always positive – i.e. you can have retrograde progress!	Achievement is different from both attainment and progress. Achievement is basically asking the following question: *Is the level the child is working at good enough when taking account of their starting point, their capability and their contextual circumstances?* Achievement is a particularly important judgement to make as it provides a real evaluation in relation to the success of the provision within your school.

THE AIM IS THAT YOU WILL BE ABLE TO MAKE A STATEMENT WHICH TICKS ALL OF THE FOLLOWING BOXES:

Where were the children when they started?

i.e. what were their **standards**.

This is called 'attainment on entry'

Where were the children when they finished?

i.e. what were their **standards**.

This is called 'attainment on exit'

The difference between these two is the **progress** they made.

What was their level of **achievement?**

In other words did they make enough progress?

Are the standards good enough?

WHAT SHOULD I LOOK AT FIRST?

There is almost too much data that we could get confused.
A suggested order for looking at your data is outlined below:

FIRST SEE PAGE 10 FOR MORE DETAILS

LOOK AT THE CONTEXTUAL INFORMATION CONTAINED IN RAISE ONLINE.

1.1.1	Basic characteristics
1.1.2	Basic characteristics by N.C. Year group
1.1.3	Ethnicity
1.1.4	Census information
1.1.5	Prior attainment of pupil in key stage 2

> This information sets the context and should inform section one of your SEF.

SECOND SEE PAGE 18 FOR MORE DETAILS

LOOK AT THE STANDARDS INFORMATION CONTAINED IN RAISE ONLINE.

5-year trend at key stage one

3.1.2	Key stage 1 overall attainment
3.1.3	Key stage 1 reading attainment
3.1.4	Key stage 1 writing attainment
3.1.5	Key stage 1 mathematics attainment
3.1.6	Key stage 1 APS trend

Latest year at key stage one

3.1.8	Percentage at each level
3.1.10	APS comparison for each pupil group

5-year trend at key stage two

3.1.11	Key stage 2 overall attainment
3.1.11	Key stage 2 English attainment
3.1.12	Key stage 2 Mathematics attainment
3.1.13	Key stage 2 Science attainment
3.1.14	Key stage 2 APS trend

Latest year at key stage two

3.1.16	Percentage at each level
3.1.18	APS comparison for each pupil group

> This information tells you how your school and pupils are performing in relation to national before taking account of any contextual factors. Any evaluation you make from this data should start, 'Attainment...' or 'Standards...'.

THIRD SEE PAGE 28 FOR MORE DETAILS

LOOK AT THE CVA INFORMATION CONTAINED IN RAISE ONLINE.

3-year CVA trend on a graph

2.1.1	Overall CVA for latest year
2.1.2	Overall CVA for last year
2.1.3	Overall CVA for year before

CVA for latest year on a graph

2.1.4	CVA for English for latest year
2.1.5	CVA for Maths for this year
2.1.6	CVA for Science for this year

3-year CVA trend in figures

2.1.7	CVA for 3 years

CVA compared to relative attainment on a graph

2.1.8	Information for this year
2.1.9	Information for last year
2.1.10	Information for year before
2.1.11	English for latest year
2.1.12	Maths for latest year
2.1.13	Science for latest year

CVA for latest year

2.1.15	CVA for pupil groups on a graph
2.1.16	CVA for pupil groups in figures
2.1.17	CVA for ethnicities
2.1.19	CVA for individual pupils on scatter-plot

> This information gives an indication of whether your outcomes are good enough when taking account of their prior attainment and contextual factors.

USING YOUR
CONTEXTUAL INFORMATION
FROM RAISE ONLINE

USING YOUR CONTEXTUAL INFORMATION FROM RAISE ONLINE

The contextual data in your RAISE online reports paints a picture of the community your serve. It gives some indicators of the type of backgrounds that your children join your school from. You should use your contextual information to supplement and support any assertions made in section one of your SEF. This initial outline and evaluation of attainment on entry is important as all other judgements made will be based on where the children enter your school.

ATTAINMENT ON ENTRY

A clear and accurate outline of attainment on entry is very important for any school. Without this, no further judgements can be made about the success and effectiveness of a school. Where children leave is irrelevant if you don't know where they entered.

You need to accurately portray the following:

- The attainment on entry

- The social and economic backgrounds of the children, including the level of prosperity or deprivation

The summary of this evaluation will appear in the school's Self Evaluation Form (SEF) and will be a basis for making all judgements about progress and achievement in your school.

ATTAINMENT ON ENTRY TIPS

- Be clear whether you are talking about attainment on entry to Nursery or Reception. In some schools this will be the same thing, in others it can be quite different. Be clear about the proportion of children that transfer from Nursery to Reception. If this is reasonably high then you can accurately talk about attainment on entry to Nursery.

- Be clear if the attainment on entry is changing, i.e. is there an overall increasing or declining trend (you will need to evidence this).

- Be specific if there is a particular cohort in the school with an attainment on entry that was significantly different from the norm.

- If appropriate, give some brief and specific details about attainment on entry of specific groups, e.g. girls, girls, ethnic groups etc.

- Give proportions of specific groups: EAL, FSM, ethnicities, ratio of boys to girls (if relevant), percentage of autumn, spring and summer birthdays, children identified with learning, social or emotional needs.

- Give brief description of the geographical location of the school and the impact this has on learners, including whether children have pre-schools experience, parental aspiration etc.

EVIDENCE BASE FOR YOUR EVALUATION OF ATTAINMENT ON ENTRY

Whatever you say about the attainment on entry of your children, needs to be backed up with evidence. The chart below shows some of the evidence that you may find helpful – though this is not exhaustive – and some schools will not require all sources others will use different or additional sources of evidence.

- Baseline information

- Foundation Stage Profile data

- Information from feeder settings

- Local authority data on levels of deprivation in your area

- 'Super output area' data from your local authority

- Information about political wards where your children live

- Social information, e.g. crime statistics, index of multiple deprivation etc

WHAT SHOULD I LOOK AT FIRST?

The following chart in your RAISE provides a quick summary of some major factors in your school.

	2004	2005	2006		20th percentile	40th percentile	60th percentile	80th percentile	
Number on roll									
School	386	357	324						
National	240	239	237	6	124	197	243	343	967
% girls									
School	47.9	47.9	47.5						
National	48.9	48.9	48.9	0.0	45.8	48.0	49.8	52.0	100.0
% of pupils known to be eligible for free school meals (FSM)									
School	73.1	60.8	62.0						
National	17.0	16.6	16.0	0.0	3.3	7.4	14.0	28.0	83.4
% of pupils from minority ethnic groups									
School	12.9	14.6	16.4						
National	17.2	15.7	20.6	0.0	2.3	4.8	9.0	22.9	100.0
% of pupils first language not / believed not to be English									
School	3.3	4.9	5.5						
National	8.4	8.9	12.5	0.0	0.0	1.1	2.9	10.7	100.0
% of pupils with a statement of SEN									
School	2.1	2.2	0.3						
National	1.7	1.7	1.6	0.0	0.4	0.9	1.5	2.4	21.6
% of pupils with SEN (including statements)									
School	15.3	15.4	15.7						
National	17.8	18.1	18.9	0.0	11.0	15.2	19.6	25.9	76.2
% attendance									
School	93.5	93.2	94.4						
National	94.5	94.6	94.2	78.9	93.2	94.1	94.8	95.5	99.7
% authorised absence									
School	5.9	5.2	4.6						
National	5.1	5.0	5.3	0.3	4.3	4.9	5.5	6.2	21.1
% unauthorised absence									
School	0.6	1.6	1.0						
National	0.4	0.4	0.5	0.0	0.0	0.1	0.3	0.7	8.3
School deprivation indicator									
School	0.6	0.6	0.6						
National	0.2	0.2	0.2	0.0	0.1	0.1	0.2	0.3	0.9

SEF TIP...

You do not need to re-write the data from this chart in sentences!

Simply use it to pick out key points that are distinctive about your school in order to back up what you are saying about the context of your children and their backgrounds.

USING THE GRAPHS ON THE PREVIOUS PAGE

The chart on the previous page shows some of the basic characteristics of your school over a 3-year period based on information from the School Level Annual Census (SLASC) and Pupils Level Annual Census (PLASC). This allows you to compares your school's key indicators against the national picture for the same period.

For each indicator the graph is divided into five sections, known as 'quintile graphs'. Each of the five sections contains approximately 20% of schools.

The following chart may put this into perspective:

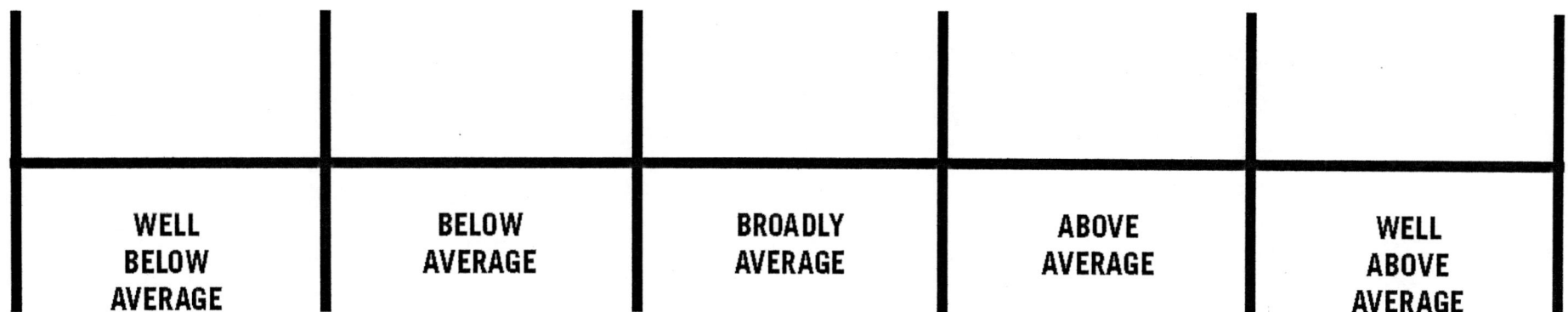

| WELL BELOW AVERAGE | BELOW AVERAGE | BROADLY AVERAGE | ABOVE AVERAGE | WELL ABOVE AVERAGE |

 Ensure that your evaluation extracts any significant changes in the context of your school over time.

USING THE SCHOOL DEPRIVATION INDICATOR AND WARD INFORMATION

The school deprivation indicator and ward information are key pieces of data that you should refer to when evaluating attainment on entry. They are indicators and only that. They do not tell the full story but do give a snapshot of your children. It is a good idea to briefly refer to both in section one of the SEF – even if you are disputing their claims!

The School Deprivation Indicator is generated from IDACI data (Income Deprivation Affecting Children Index). This data comes from the Office of the Deputy Prime Minister and is linked to work on Index of Multiple Deprivation and Super Output Areas.

The School Deprivation Indicator shows the percentage of children in each super output area that live in families that are income deprived (i.e. in receipt of Income Support, Income based Jobseeker's Allowance, Working Families' Tax Credit or Disabled Person's Tax Credit below a given threshold). An IDACI score of, for example, 0.19 means that 19% of children aged less than 16 in that super output area are living in families that are income deprived.

At the time of writing, an IDACI rating of 0.14 was average.

If you compare the two extracts below you will see this in real terms:

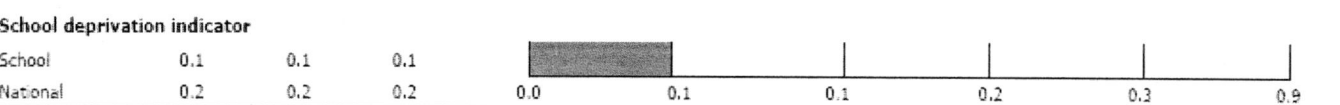

A school with a significantly high degree of deprivation	School deprivation indicator								
	School	0.6	0.6	0.6					
	National	0.2	0.2	0.2	0.0	0.1	0.1	0.2	0.3	0.9

A school with a low degree of deprivation	School deprivation indicator								
	School	0.1	0.1	0.1					
	National	0.2	0.2	0.2	0.0	0.1	0.1	0.2	0.3	0.9

Ward information again gives a broad picture of the places the children come from. Remember that political wards are not homogeneous and as result may not present a good indicator of your children's attainment on entry. Remember to refer to this data in your SEF – stating whether you agree of disagree with it. Compare the following two extracts:

This ward information paints a picture of children from backgrounds in an area of deprivation in an inner city.

% Pupils in ward	% Adult higher education	% High social class households	% Minority ethnic children	% Over-crowded households
62.1	11.3	10.3	25.2	17.4
28.7	9.7	10.2	19.0	12.8
5.0	5.8	7.3	4.5	16.9
1.5	9.4	12.7	3.6	11.0
1.2	25.1	14.0	48.4	23.1
0.6	13.1	19.0	4.2	8.7
0.3	28.2	22.2	46.3	11.7
0.3	34.9	27.5	20.1	9.0
0.3	9.3	12.3	5.5	11.4
	19.8	20.7	10.3	15.1

This ward information paints a picture of children from an area of considerable affluence.

% Pupils in ward	% Adult higher education	% High social class households	% Minority ethnic children	% Over-crowded households
43.5	27.8	31.5	4.3	1.9
30.9	30.0	33.2	6.2	1.9
9.4	24.3	24.6	3.9	3.4
2.6	22.2	22.4	0.9	5.5
2.6	24.8	27.6	6.5	4.4
2.1	7.6	11.2	1.6	14.5
2.1	19.3	19.3	1.9	7.6
1.6	8.8	9.9	1.3	6.6
1.6	18.7	23.7	2.6	3.4
1.0	16.0	21.4	2.4	5.2
	19.8	20.7	10.3	15.1

TWO CONTRASTING EXAMPLES OF ATTAINMENT ON ENTRY STATEMENTS FROM REAL SCHOOLS

1

Whilst our children some from a variety of backgrounds, our overall attainment on entry is below average. This is supported by both ward information and the school deprivation indicator.

On entry to reception, children are assessed as being below national expectations in all six areas of learning. Our assessments, based on FSP points, show that children are overall between points 1 and 2. Of the six areas, the weakest areas are CLL and PSED.

Almost half our children some from homes where English is the first language. The main languages represented are Urdu, Punjabi and Sylhetti (the latter is an entirely oral language with no written form).

Children join the reception class from a wide variety of settings (nine settings this year). This results in a lack of consistency in assessment information. On average, about 50% of children have had some pre-school experience. The remaining children are usually cared for in the home, often by extended family members.

The level of deprivation in the area is high and this is recognised in both local authority and national data. There are a variety of community initiatives which are aiming to encourage parents to support and value schools. Previously, many parents demonstrated a 'distant' attitude to school often linked to their own personal experiences.

2

Whilst our children come from a variety of backgrounds, our attainment on entry is broadly average. This is supported by our contextual data and Foundation Stage 'on entry' data.

There are no significant differences on entry between the six areas of learning. However, within CLL children enter below average in relation to the 'writing aspects'. Children enter 'slightly above' in relation to KUW.

The vast majority of our pupils come from homes where English is the first language. We often welcome traveller children who live on the local authority site near the school. We have two traveller pupils who have remained at the school. Over the past year, we have admitted a further six traveller pupils who have subsequently moved to other areas of the country.

Mobility, whilst broadly average, has increased over the past three years. This is due to upwardly mobile families who wish to relocate to 'more prosperous' areas of the city.

The majority of our children enter reception with some pre-school experience. This is mainly in two local settings (one maintained, one non-maintained).

REMEMBER: There is no one way to write an attainment on entry statement. These are simply examples.

WHATEVER YOU WRITE: Must accurately reflect your school and your children; and be able to be backed up with evidence.

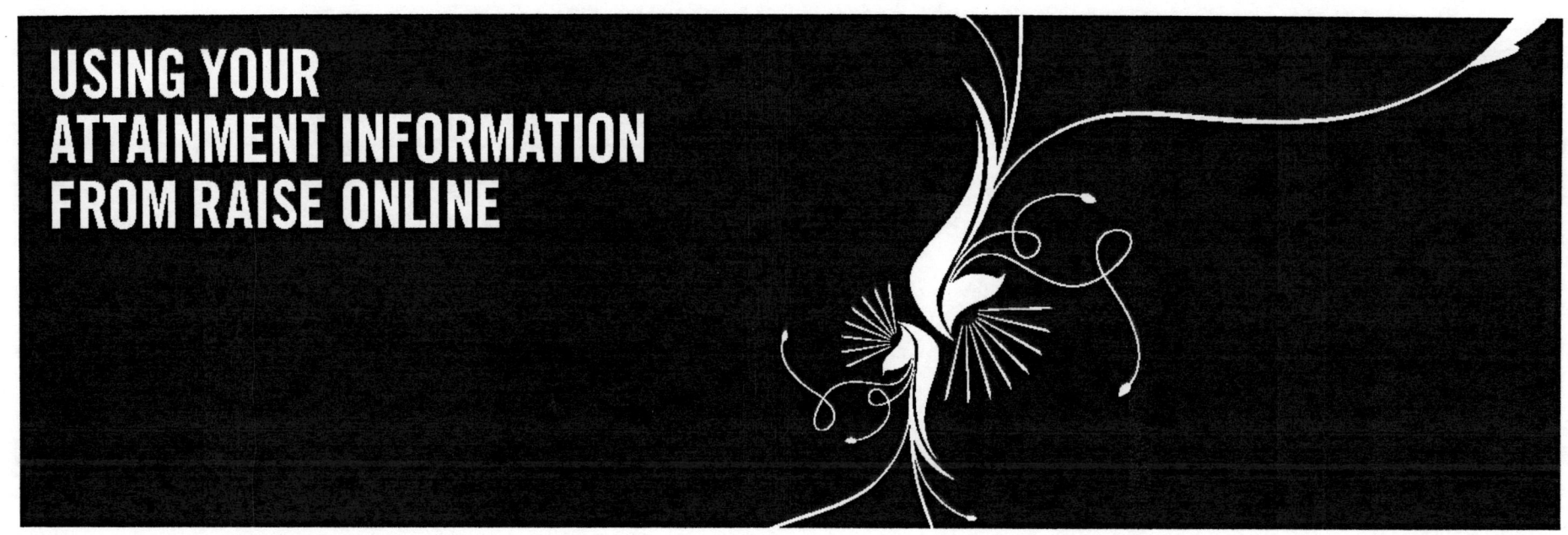

USING YOUR ATTAINMENT INFORMATION FROM RAISE ONLINE

USING YOUR ATTAINMENT INFORMATION

To be absolutely clear...

... in a school improvement context, attainment and standards refer to the same thing.

When we refer to either of these, we are talking about a judgement in relation to nationally agreed expectations.

In the case of primary schools, we are looking at how we compare to both national expectations and national averages by the end of key stage one and key stage two.

RAISE online does this comparison through the use of average point scores (APS). You need to be familiar with APS in order to use this information quickly. If don't already do so, it is well worth considering using APS in your own in-school tracking. This means that you are talking the same language as RAISE online and can make easy comparisons about whether all year groups are on-track to reach agreed targets.

The chart on the next page shows the average point scores allocated to each national curriculum level.

The easiest way to remember average point scores is to remember the numbers attached to the following two national expectations:

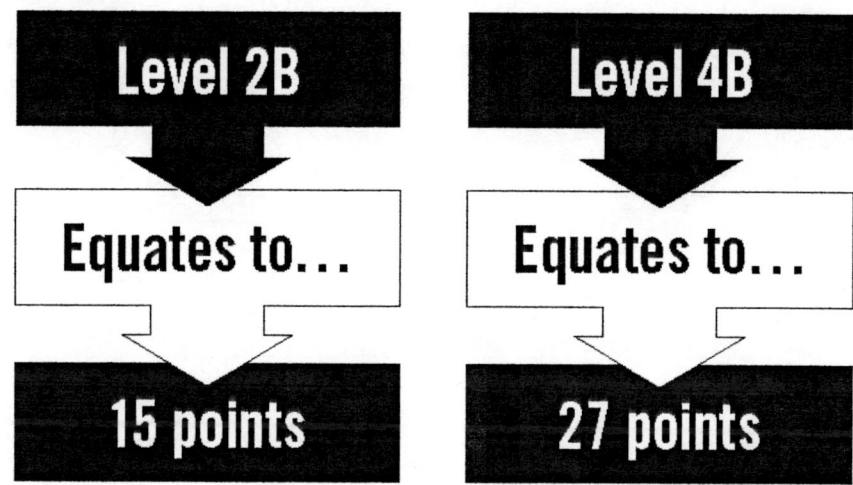

Level 2B	Level 4B
Equates to...	Equates to...
15 points	27 points

AVERAGE POINT SCORES (APS)

National curriculum levels can be converted into point scores. When the national curriculum was designed, the expected progress for the median pupil (the one who was exactly in the middle of the national ability range) was one level in two years, with higher attainers progressing more rapidly and lower attainers at a slower rate. Each level is equivalent to 6 points. So 6 points represents two years, or 6 terms, of progress for the median pupil. Therefore each point represents (approximately) one term's progress.

Expected levels by the end of each key stage

Key stage 1:
level 2 (15 points)

Key stage 2:
level 4 (27 points)

Key stage 3:
level 5.5 (36 points)

N.C. LEVEL	EQUIVALENT POINT SCORE
W	3
Level 1C	7
Level 1 (1B)	**9**
Level 1A	11
Level 2C	13
Level 2 (2B)	**15**
Level 2A	17
Level 3C	19
Level 3 (3B)	**21**
Level 3A	23
Level 4C	25
Level 4 (4B)	**27**
Level 4A	29
Level 5C	31
Level 5 (5B)	**33**
Level 5A	35
Level 6C	37
Level 6 (6B)	**39**
Level 6A	41

KNOWING HOW YOU DIFFER FROM NATIONAL BASED ON AVERAGE POINT SCORE (I.E. ATTAINMENT)

Given what you know about average point scores it is easy to then consider, *'How different are we from the national picture?'*

You must answer this question with caution. Many people take 'national' to mean 15 points at the end of KS1 or 27 points at the end of KS2. Remember that this is an expectation rather than the national average.

In order to look for your difference from the national - use the information in RAISE on-line to compare your end of key stage APS to the national for the same year.

Year		2001	2002	2003	2004	2005
All Subjects	Cohort	29	22	29	25	29
	School	13.2	11.7 ↓	12.3 ↑	14.9 ↑	14.2
	National	15.3	15.5	15.5	15.6	15.4
	Difference	-2.1	-3.8	-3.2	-0.7	-1.3
KS1	Significance	Sig-	Sig-			Sig-

These figures show the ACTUAL difference between your attainment and the national based on APS

Year		2001	2002	2003	2004	2005
All Subjects	Cohort	28	28	25	29	28
	School	28.9	28.7	28.6	27.8	26.0
	National	27.0	27.3	27.4	27.5	27.6
	Difference	1.9	1.4	1.2	0.3	-1.6
KS2	Significance	Sig+	Sig+	Sig+		Sig-

WHAT DO YOU DO WITH THIS STANDARDS INFORMATION?

Having worked out how different you are from the national picture, you need to decide what this means. Ofsted give some guidance on this. These figures are part of a judgment called 'determining educational importance'.

Ofsted tell us what constitutes 'exceptional performance' at the end of a key stage in relation to attainment.

- At the end of KS1 exceptional performance is 2 points different from the national APS.

- At the end of KS2 exceptional performance is 2.5 points different from the national APS.

Put simply, this means that...

If your standards are above the difference (from national) your standards are more likely to be deemed as 'outstanding'.

If your standards are below the difference (from national) your standards are more likely to be deemed 'inadequate'.

Remember that at this point we are only considering attainment outcomes and have not factored in the backgrounds or context of the pupils in your school.

At Key Stage 1

Year		2002	2003	2004	2005	2006
All Subjects	Cohort	30	28	32	28	26
	School	14.0	14.3	12.6 ↓	13.3	15.5 ↑
	National	15.5	15.5	15.6	15.4	15.3
	Difference	-1.5	-1.2	-3.0	-2.1	0.2
	Significance	Sig-	Sig-	Sig-	Sig-	
Reading	Cohort	30	28	32	28	26
	School	14.1	14.6	12.5	13.8	16.2 ↑
	National	15.8	15.7	15.8	15.8	15.7
	Difference	-1.7	-1.1	-3.3	-2.0	0.5
	Significance	Sig-		Sig-	Sig-	
Writing	Cohort	30	28	32	28	26
	School	13.2	13.3	11.9	12.3	14.8 ↑
	National	14.4	14.6	14.6	14.6	14.5
	Difference	-1.2	-1.3	-2.7	-2.3	0.3
	Significance			Sig-	Sig-	
Mathematics	Cohort	30	28	32	28	26
	School	14.5	15.0	13.6	13.9	15.4
	National	16.5	16.3	16.3	16.0	15.8
	Difference	-2.0	-1.3	-2.7	-2.1	-0.4
	Significance	Sig-		Sig-	Sig-	

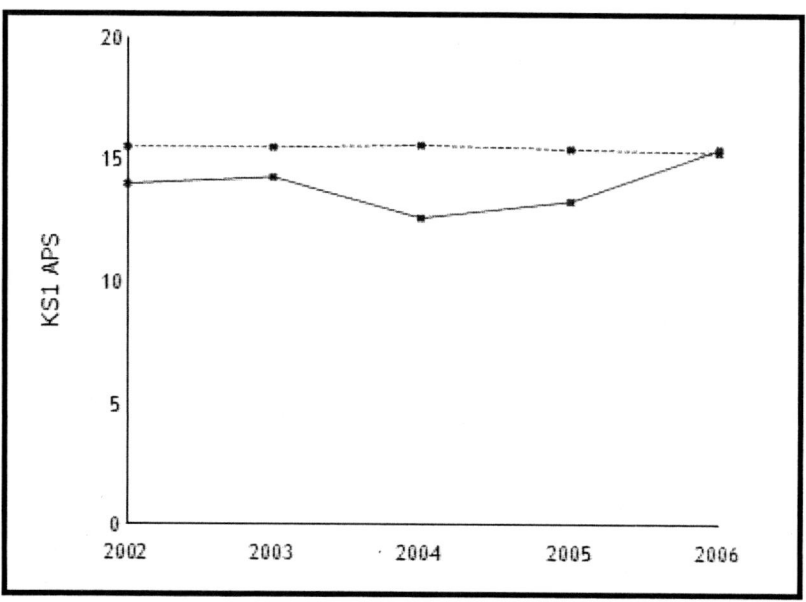

By the end of key stage one, standards are below and sometimes well below national expectations. In 2004 and 2005 standards were inadequate as judged by Ofsted's educational importance criteria.

Standards improved in 2006 due to ...

At Key Stage 2

Year		2002	2003	2004	2005	2006
All Subjects	Cohort	102	87	75	26	28
	School	27.9	29.0	28.7	28.8	29.7
	National	27.3	27.4	27.5	27.8	27.9
	Difference	0.6	1.6	1.2	1.0	1.8
	Significance		Sig+	Sig+		Sig+
English	Cohort	34	29	25	27	28
	School	28.4	28.9	27.5	28.6	29.4
	National	27.0	26.8	26.9	26.8	27.4
	Difference	1.4	2.1	0.6	1.8	2.0
	Significance		Sig+			Sig+
Mathematics	Cohort	34	29	25	27	28
	School	27.0	27.8	28.0	27.9	28.7
	National	26.7	26.8	27.0	26.9	27.3
	Difference	0.3	1.0	1.0	1.0	1.4
	Significance					
Science	Cohort	34	29	25	27	28
	School	28.2	30.3	30.6	30.0	31.1
	National	28.3	28.6	28.6	28.7	28.9
	Difference	-0.1	1.7	2.0	1.3	2.2
	Significance			Sig+		Sig+

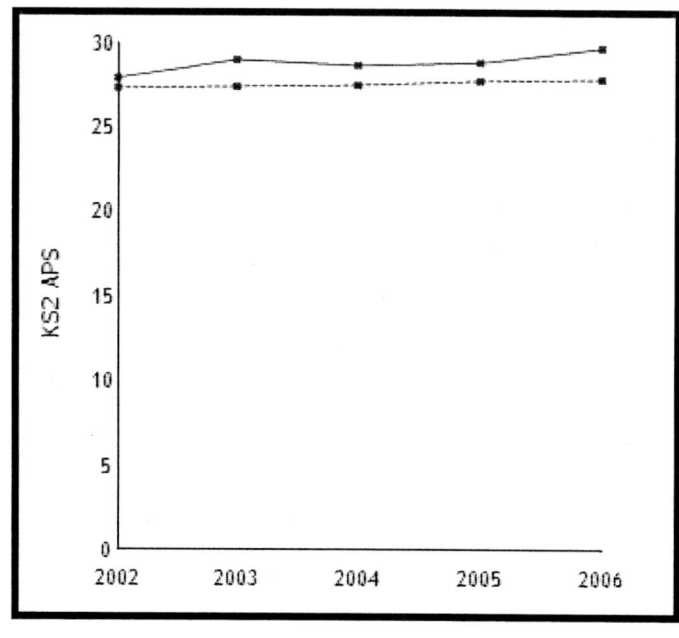

By the end of key stage two, standards are above average (but not well above).

STATISTICAL SIGNIFICANCE IN RELATION TO STANDARDS

Your RAISE online will make use of the following symbols:

 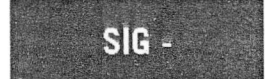

Basically, all these show is where you fit in the national 'pecking order'.

Statistical significance is calculated annually:

- It is calculated around a standard deviation test

- This looks at your spread of results around the mean and compares them to the national picture

- It is possible to have similar figures for subjects and find sig+/- for one subject and not another. This is because the mean for each subject is different.

In many ways this doesn't tell us a lot.

If you are 'sig +', you are in the top group of schools based on standards (roughly the top 30%).
i.e. your results are above average

If you are neither 'sig +' not 'sig –' your results are in the average group.

If you are 'sig –' you are in the bottom group of schools based on standards (roughly the bottom 30%).
i.e. your results are below average

The biggest problem with these indicators is that they do not indicate where within the bottom 30% of schools you are, i.e. you could be just within the bottom 30% or a very long way within the bottom 30%.

REMEMBER – whilst this is an indicator, it needs to be viewed alongside your progress and CVA data to give a much fuller picture of the effectiveness of your school.

DIGGING A LITTLE DEEPER WITH STANDARDS

The standards information about pupil groups should be used to identify any key issues relating to standards by the end of KS1 and KS2. Like with the contextual information, do not simply re-write the data in sentences. Use the data as a basis for pulling out important points about where children do well or need to improve their standards.

SOME QUESTIONS TO CONSIDER

- What does your APS tell you in relation to national expectations?

- What does your APS tell you in relation to the national average(s)?

- Are you sig+/sig-?

- What is the trend over time?

- What is the difference between subjects? (APS may look OK overall but be stronger/weaker in a specific subject)

- Is there a difference of 2 points or more by the end of KS1? (if so this is educationally important)

- Can you convincingly explain any apparent 'blips' in attainment?

Consider the above questions in relation to:

- Gender

- FSM/non-FSM

- EAL/non-EAL

- SEN/non-SEN/school action/school action plus/statements

- Ethnicity

- Term of birth

- Other significant and/or vulnerable groups in your school

Use the attainment thresholds to:

- Compare percentages in order to evaluate whether there are enough pupils attaining at the higher level.

- Use KS1 standards data to decide what KS2 projections will look like.

LOOKING TO THE FUTURE WITH YOUR STANDARDS

A major problem with RAISE online is that it is reporting on pupils who have left your school. Some of the data in a primary school RAISE online refers to pupils who are now in year 9 at secondary school. Whilst the school is responsible for this data and has to take ownership of it; it is also important to look forward.

By using your own in-school tracking data – made even easier if you use average point scores, you can compare your data to two things:

- the national trend over time

- your own school trend over time

By doing this, you are then well able to ascertain how well on track your children are to hit or indeed exceed targets and past performance.

Whilst you can make this a year-on-year exercise it is definitely worth doing at the end of year 4, i.e. half way through key stage 2. This gives a good amount of time to ensure that provision is meeting the needs of the cohort.

USING THIS EVIDENCE DURING INSPECTION

If you were to use this kind of evidence to show inspectors that achievement is possibly better now than it has been in the past, it would be essential that you could support this by other evidence. A key piece of evidence would be ongoing scrutiny of children's work alongside discussion with children.

If successful, this evidence, alongside your tracking, could support the view that children are on-track to reach challenging targets.

USING YOUR
C.V.A. INFORMATION
FROM RAISE ONLINE

CONTEXTUAL VALUE ADDED

Your contextual value added (CVA) data is calculated by:

Taking a child's prior attainment, i.e. their levels in reading, writing and maths at key stage one

Taking the same child's levels at the end of key stage two in English, mathematics and science

Calculating their value added compared to similar children nationally (based on the progress made by the median child in the same cohort)

In 2006 the breakdown of CVA in schools nationally was:

Top 5%	**102.1+**
Next 25%	**100.9 – 102.0**
Next 15%	**100.3 – 100.8**
Middle 20%	**99.8 – 100.2**
Next 15%	**99.3 – 99.7**
Next 20%	**98.0 – 99.2**
Bottom 5%	**97.9**

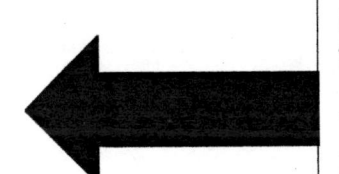

This then gives each child an individual contextual value added score which combine to make the overall CVA score for the school.

This score is centred around 100. A CVA of 100 shows that every child has made the 'expected progress' when taking account of their prior attainment and context.

Factor in the impact that their context plays in their progress based on national data.
Taking account of:

• Gender
• SEN
• When they joined the school
• Term of birth
• Deprivation
• Ethnicity (linked to FSM)
• EAL (linked to prior attainment)

KNOWING HOW TO USE CVA DATA

CVA data offers a picture of how well children have achieved in relation to both their starting points (prior attainment) and their contextual features, such as gender, age, ethnicity etc.

Primary phase CVA is centred around 100.

Your RAISE on-line report outlines three CVA outcomes:

> You need to use this information to make an evaluation in order to answer the question: How well do pupils achieve?
> As with attainment data, Ofsted give guidance on how to use CVA data.

Overall CVA	For example...	**Overall contextual value added**
		This report provides the overall contextual value added measure for particular groups within the school relative to the national mean of 100. The school is placed within the national distribution to illustrate the range of contextual value added scores attained by other mainstream maintained schools.

	Cohort	CVA School Score	95% Confidence Interval	Significance
All pupils	26	100.4	0.7	

| CVA for subjects | For example... | | | | | | | |

		Contextual Value Added			CVA By Subject 2005		
	Number of pupils in latest year	2003	2004	2005	English	Maths	Science
All Pupils	26	-	101.1	100.4	99.9	100.5	100.7

| CVA for pupil groups | For example... |

	All pupils	Girls	Boys	Girls < Level 2	Girls at Level 2	Girls > Level 2	Boys < Level 2	Boys at Level 2	Boys > Level 2	Non-FSM	FSM	Non-SEN	SEN: Non-statement	SEN: Statement	First Language: English	First Language: Other	Not In Care	In Care
Cohort	26	8	18	2.0	6.0	-	7.0	11.0	-	19.0	7.0	19.0	7.0	-	11.0	15.0	26.0	-
School score	100.4	100.3	100.5	100.3	100.1	-	99.7	100.9	-	100.1	101.1	100.6	99.9	-	100.5	100.3	100.4	-
95% confidence interval	0.9	1.2	0.9	1.7	1.3	-	1.2	1.1	-	0.8	1.2	0.8	1.2	-	1.1	0.9	0.7	-
Significance						-			-					-				-

These figures are part of a judgment called

'determining educational importance'.

Ofsted tell us what constitutes 'exceptional performance' at the end of key stage 2 in relation to CVA.

At the end of KS2 exceptional performance is 1.5 points different from 100.

Put simply, this means that…

If your CVA is 101.5 or greater, achievement is more likely to be deemed **'outstanding'**.

If your CVA is 98.5 or less, achievement is more likely to be deemed **'inadequate'**.

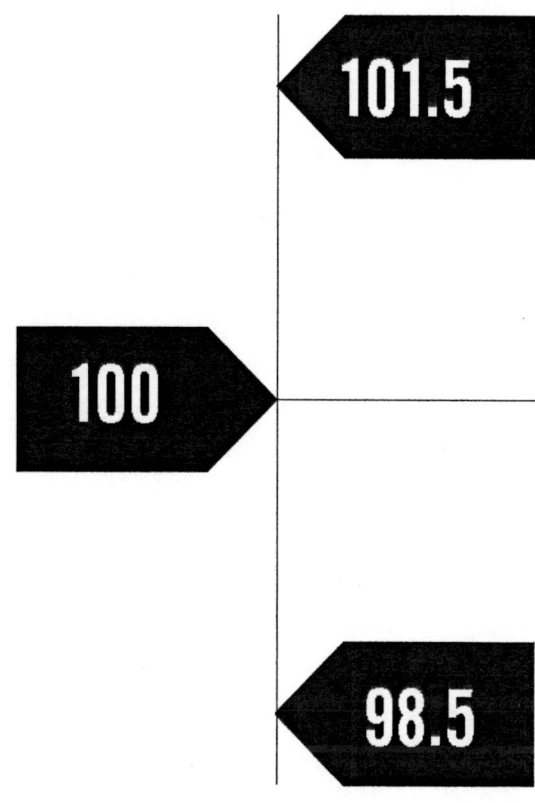

CONFIDENCE INTERVALS

The DfES offer the following explanation of confidence intervals (Guide to contextual value added – Dec 2006).

> **We can use the contextual value added score as a measure of school effectiveness, but as with 'simple' value added it is based only on a set of pupils' results for a particular test paper on a particular day.**
>
> **The school could have been equally effective and yet the same set of pupils might have achieved different results on the day. And the school would almost certainly have shown slightly different results with a different set of pupils, even with the same levels of prior attainment. Hence, although the contextual value added score is based on all pupil in the school cohort (not just a sample of them), this degree of uncertainty should be taken into account if interpreting the figures as estimates of a school's effectiveness.**
>
> **The uncertainty of a contextual value added score as a measure of school effectiveness can be presented as a confidence interval. This is a range of scores within which we can be statistically confident that the 'true' school effectiveness will lie. The size of the confidence interval is determined by the number of pupils in your calculation.**

At the risk of getting technical, it is important to have some understanding of confidence intervals. Ofsted build your RAISE on-line report to a 95% level of confidence, in other words they are 95% certain that the CVA is in the right place but there is a chance it is within the range given.

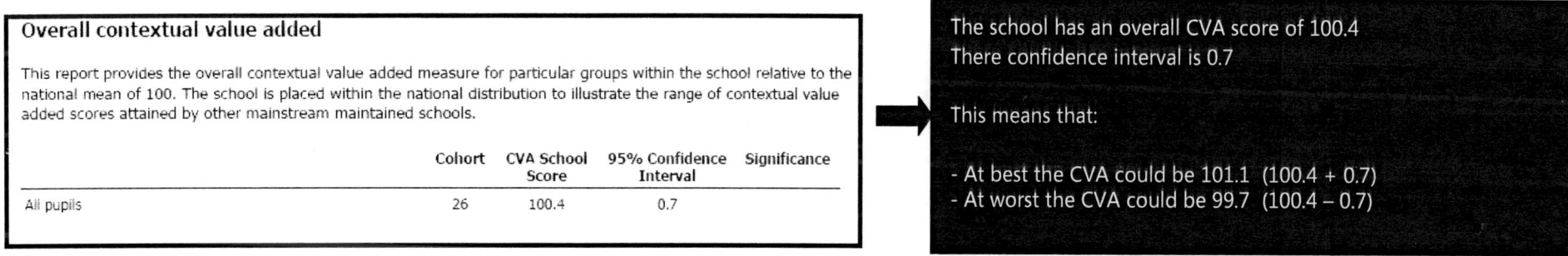

Overall contextual value added

This report provides the overall contextual value added measure for particular groups within the school relative to the national mean of 100. The school is placed within the national distribution to illustrate the range of contextual value added scores attained by other mainstream maintained schools.

	Cohort	CVA School Score	95% Confidence Interval	Significance
All pupils	26	100.4	0.7	

The school has an overall CVA score of 100.4
There confidence interval is 0.7

This means that:

- At best the CVA could be 101.1 (100.4 + 0.7)
- At worst the CVA could be 99.7 (100.4 – 0.7)

For CVA, the size of the confidence interval depends on the number of pupils in the cohort. Where the interval is narrow, the cohort is large; where it is wide, the cohort is small.

Confidence intervals are displayed like this:

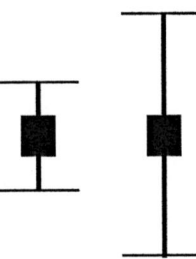

Confidence interval graphs show your school's position compared to the national position (see below):

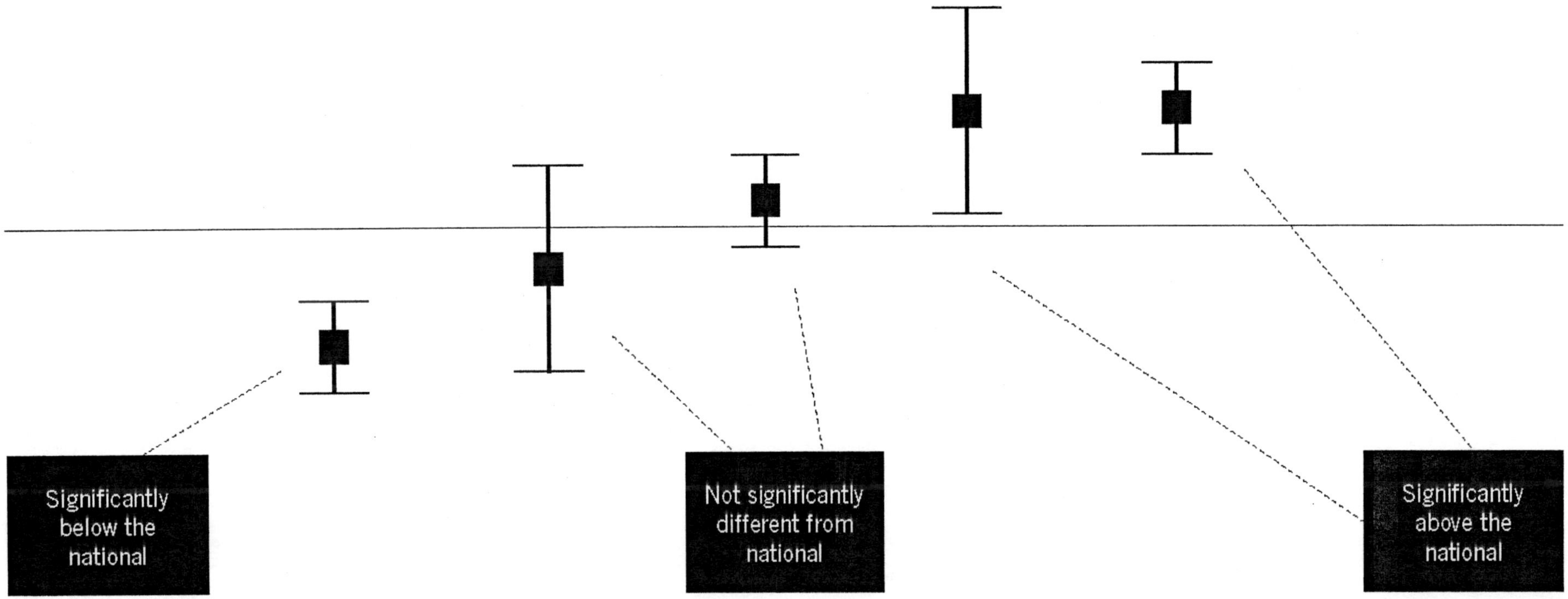

Significantly
below the
national

Not significantly
different from
national

Significantly
above the
national

WHAT DOES SIG+ OR SIG- MEAN IN RELATION TO PROGRESS?

SIG +	THE TOP 25% OF SCHOOLS
	THE MIDDLE 50% OF SCHOOLS
SIG -	THE BOTTOM 25% OF SCHOOLS

(Note: the fact that a school has sig+ CVA distinguishes it from those with sig- or not significant CVA, but does not distinguish it from the other 25% of schools that also have sig+ CVA.]

A more helpful place to look to see how you compare to other schools is your percentile rank, the following pages explain this...

PERCENTILE RANK

The percentile rank rating indicates how you fare when compared to all other primary schools in England. This comparison is based on your CVA ratings – i.e. when they have already levelled the playing field by taken account of the specific contextual factors of the children in your cohort.

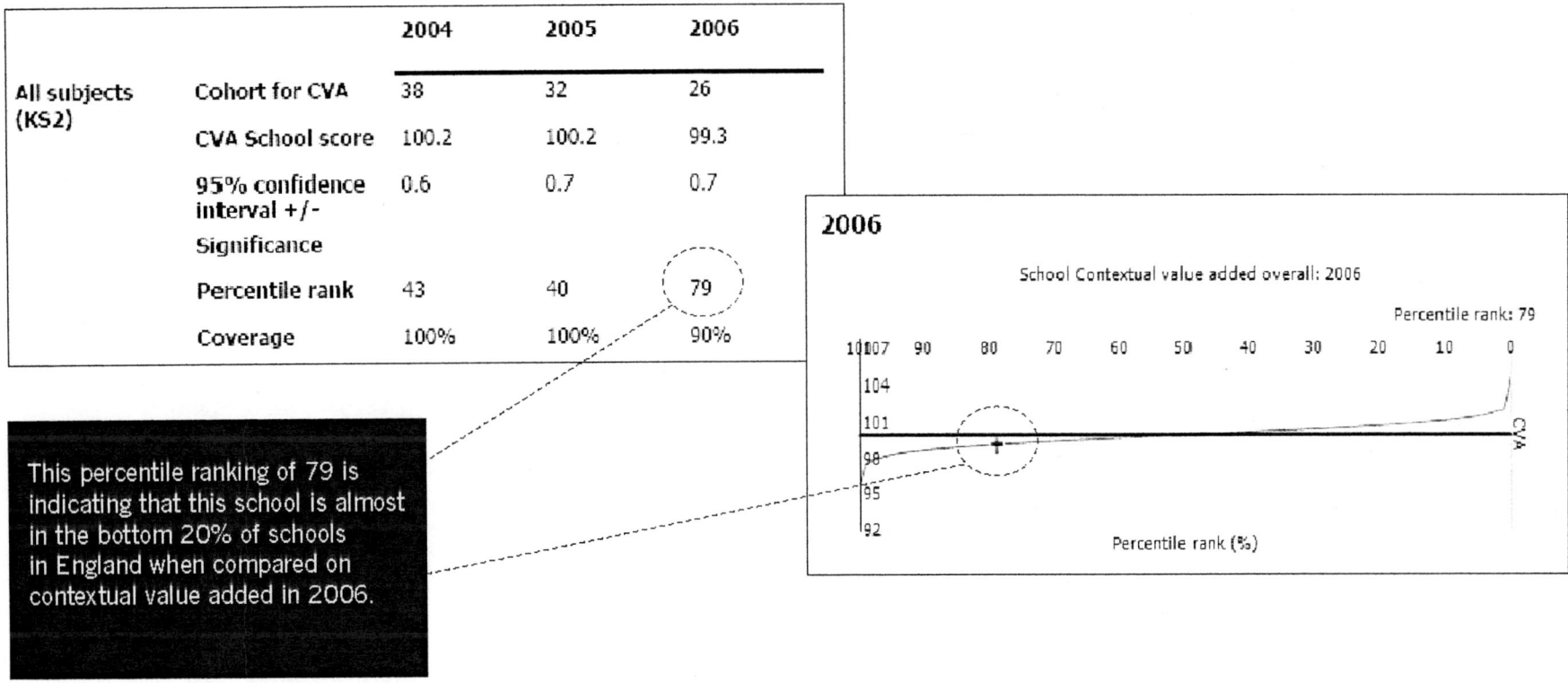

		2004	2005	2006
All subjects (KS2)	Cohort for CVA	38	32	26
	CVA School score	100.2	100.2	99.3
	95% confidence interval +/-	0.6	0.7	0.7
	Significance			
	Percentile rank	43	40	79
	Coverage	100%	100%	90%

This percentile ranking of 79 is indicating that this school is almost in the bottom 20% of schools in England when compared on contextual value added in 2006.

2006

School Contextual value added overall: 2006

Percentile rank: 79

Percentile rank (%)

IDENTIFYING UNDER ACHIEVEMENT

One of the specific points asked in the SEF is whether there is any under-achievement in the school? Ofsted interpret this on three levels:

i. **WHOLE SCHOOL**

ii. **SUBJECTS**

iii. **PUPIL GROUPS**

So, you need to be clear in your analysis whether there is any underachievement in any of the above. So even if the CVA is positive overall, you must also be confident that deeper analysis does not identify other types of under-achievement.

Places to look to test this out are...

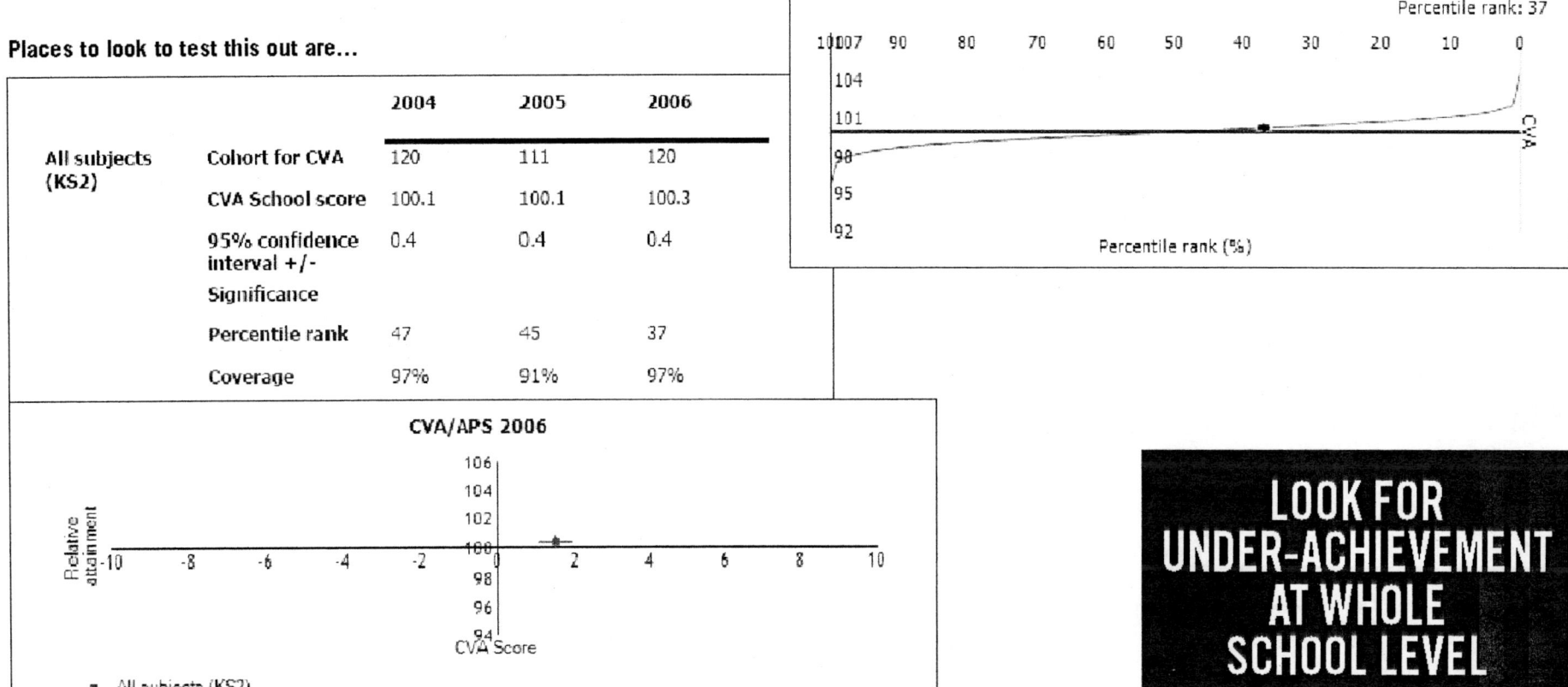

		2004	2005	2006
All subjects (KS2)	Cohort for CVA	120	111	120
	CVA School score	100.1	100.1	100.3
	95% confidence interval +/-	0.4	0.4	0.4
	Significance			
	Percentile rank	47	45	37
	Coverage	97%	91%	97%

Percentile rank: 37

CVA/APS 2006

- All subjects (KS2)

LOOK FOR UNDER-ACHIEVEMENT AT WHOLE SCHOOL LEVEL

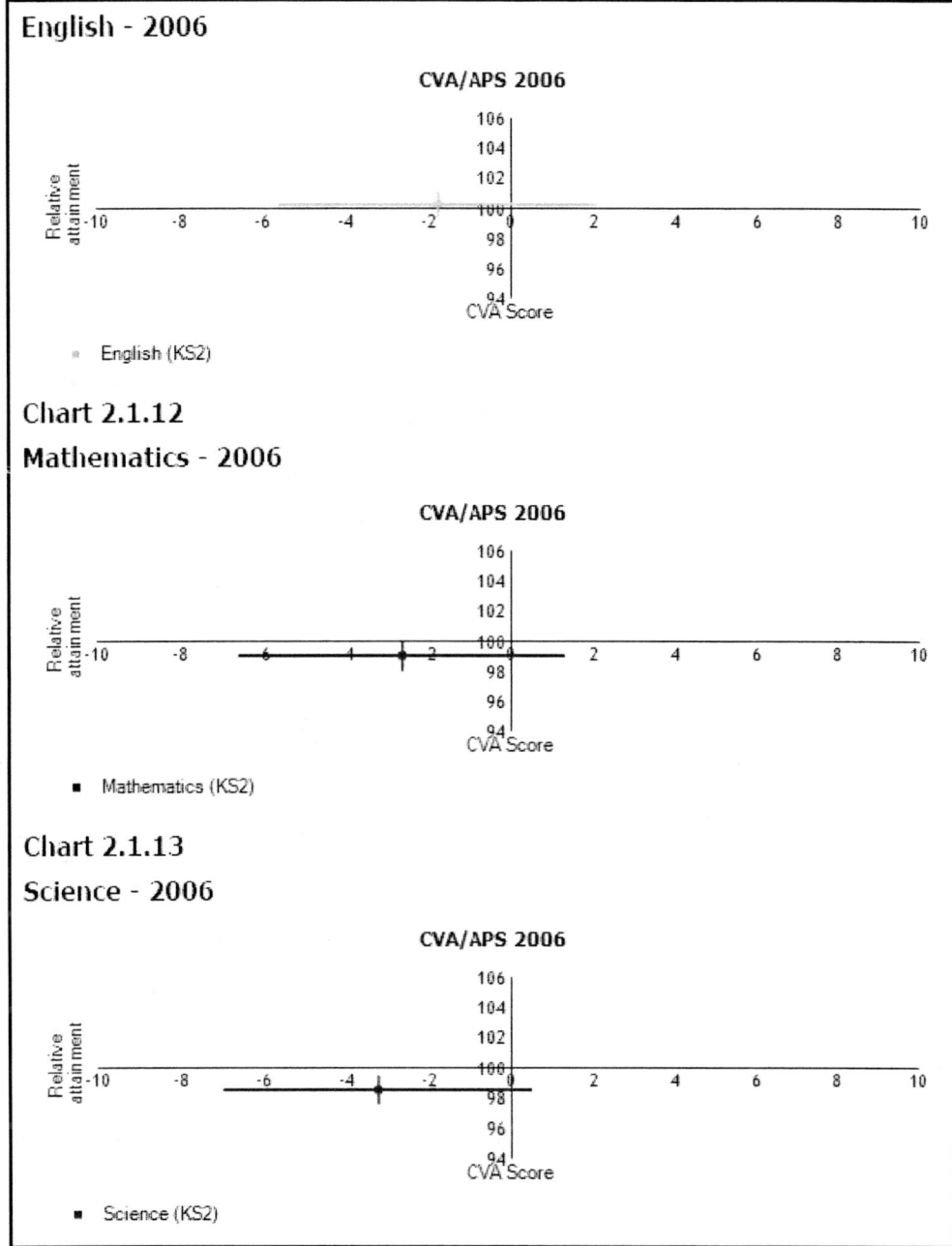

English - 2006

CVA/APS 2006

English (KS2)

Chart 2.1.12

Mathematics - 2006

CVA/APS 2006

Mathematics (KS2)

Chart 2.1.13

Science - 2006

CVA/APS 2006

Science (KS2)

LOOK FOR UNDER-ACHIEVEMENT AT SUBJECT LEVEL

English (KS2)	Cohort for CVA	38	32	26
	CVA School score	100.2	100.2	100.3
	95% confidence interval +/-	0.7	0.7	0.8
	Significance			
	Percentile rank	44	38	38
	Coverage	100%	100%	90%
Mathematics (KS2)	Cohort for CVA	38	32	26
	CVA School score	100.8	100.9	99.0 ↓
	95% confidence interval +/-	0.9	0.9	1.0
	Significance		Sig+	
	Percentile rank	28	20	82
	Coverage	100%	100%	90%
Science (KS2)	Cohort for CVA	38	32	26
	CVA School score	99.7	99.5	98.5
	95% confidence interval +/-	0.8	0.9	0.9
	Significance			Sig-
	Percentile rank	63	69	92
	Coverage	100%	100%	90%

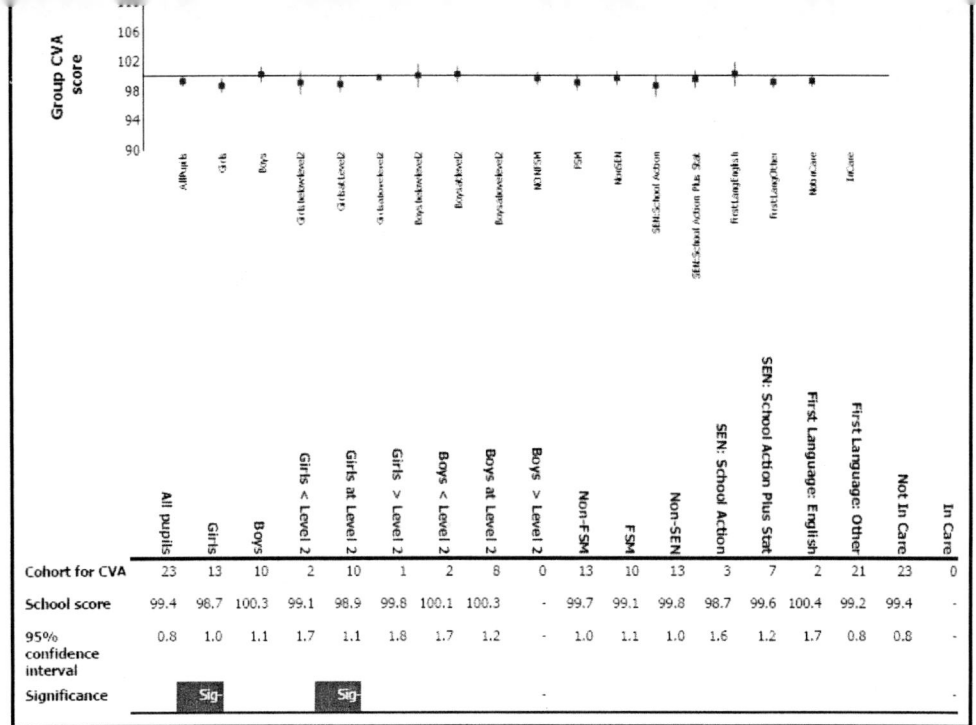

	All pupils	Girls	Boys	Girls < Level 2	Girls at Level 2	Girls > Level 2	Boys < Level 2	Boys at Level 2	Boys > Level 2	Non-FSM	FSM	Non-SEN	SEN: School Action	SEN: School Action Plus Stat	First Language: English	First Language: Other	Not In Care	In Care
Cohort for CVA	23	13	10	2	10	1	2	8	0	13	10	13	3	7	2	21	23	0
School score	99.4	98.7	100.3	99.1	98.9	99.8	100.1	100.3	-	99.7	99.1	99.8	98.7	99.6	100.4	99.2	99.4	-
95% confidence interval	0.8	1.0	1.1	1.7	1.1	1.8	1.7	1.2	-	1.0	1.1	1.0	1.6	1.2	1.7	0.8	0.8	-
Significance		Sig-			Sig-										-			-

LOOK FOR UNDER-ACHIEVEMENT AT PUPIL LEVEL

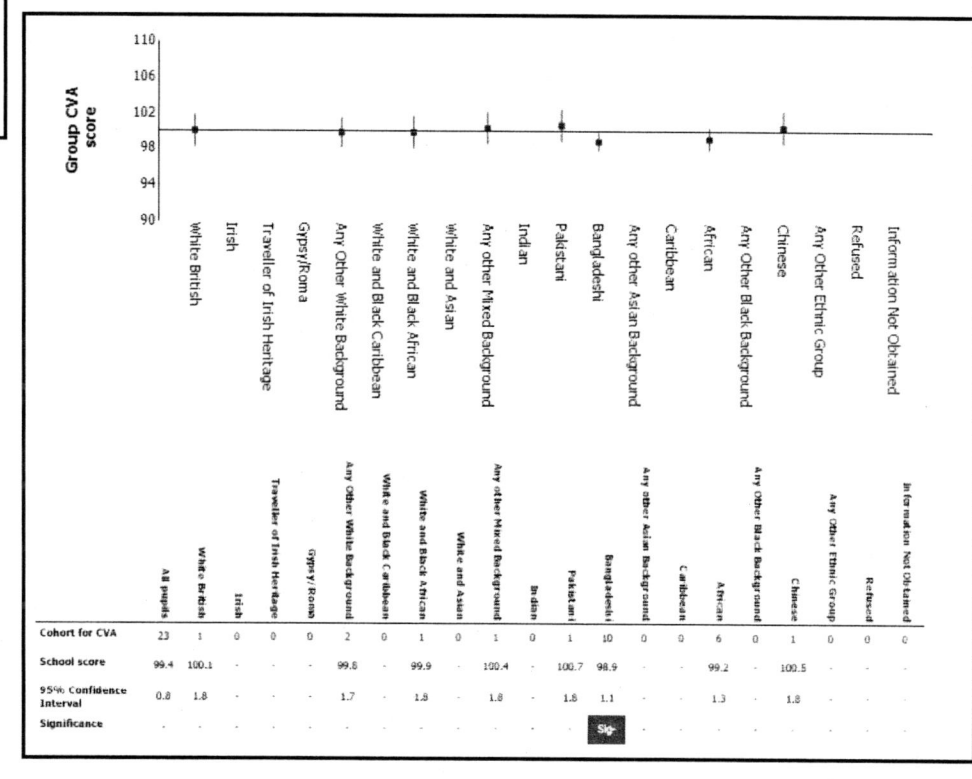

	All pupils	White British	Irish	Traveller of Irish Heritage	Gypsy/Roma	Any Other White Background	White and Black Caribbean	White and Black African	White and Asian	Any other Mixed Background	Indian	Pakistani	Bangladeshi	Any other Asian Background	Caribbean	African	Any Other Black Background	Chinese	Any Other Ethnic Group	Refused	Information Not Obtained
Cohort for CVA	23	1	0	0	0	2	0	1	0	1	0	1	10	0	0	6	0	1	0	0	0
School score	99.4	100.1	-	-	-	99.8	-	99.9	-	100.4	-	100.7	98.9	-	-	99.2	-	100.5	-	-	-
95% Confidence Interval	0.8	1.8	-	-	-	1.7	-	1.8	-	1.8	-	1.8	1.1	-	-	1.3	-	1.8	-	-	-
Significance	-	-	-	-	-	-	-	-	-	-	-		Sig-	-	-	-	-	-	-	-	-

USING THE SCATTER-PLOT GRAPH

The scatter plot graph can be used for two main things:

1. identifying an overall picture of pupil achievement in the cohort
2. identifying who specific children are in order to 'dig a little deeper'

Given that this graph is generated by using CVA data it has already levelled the playing field by taking a range of factors into account.

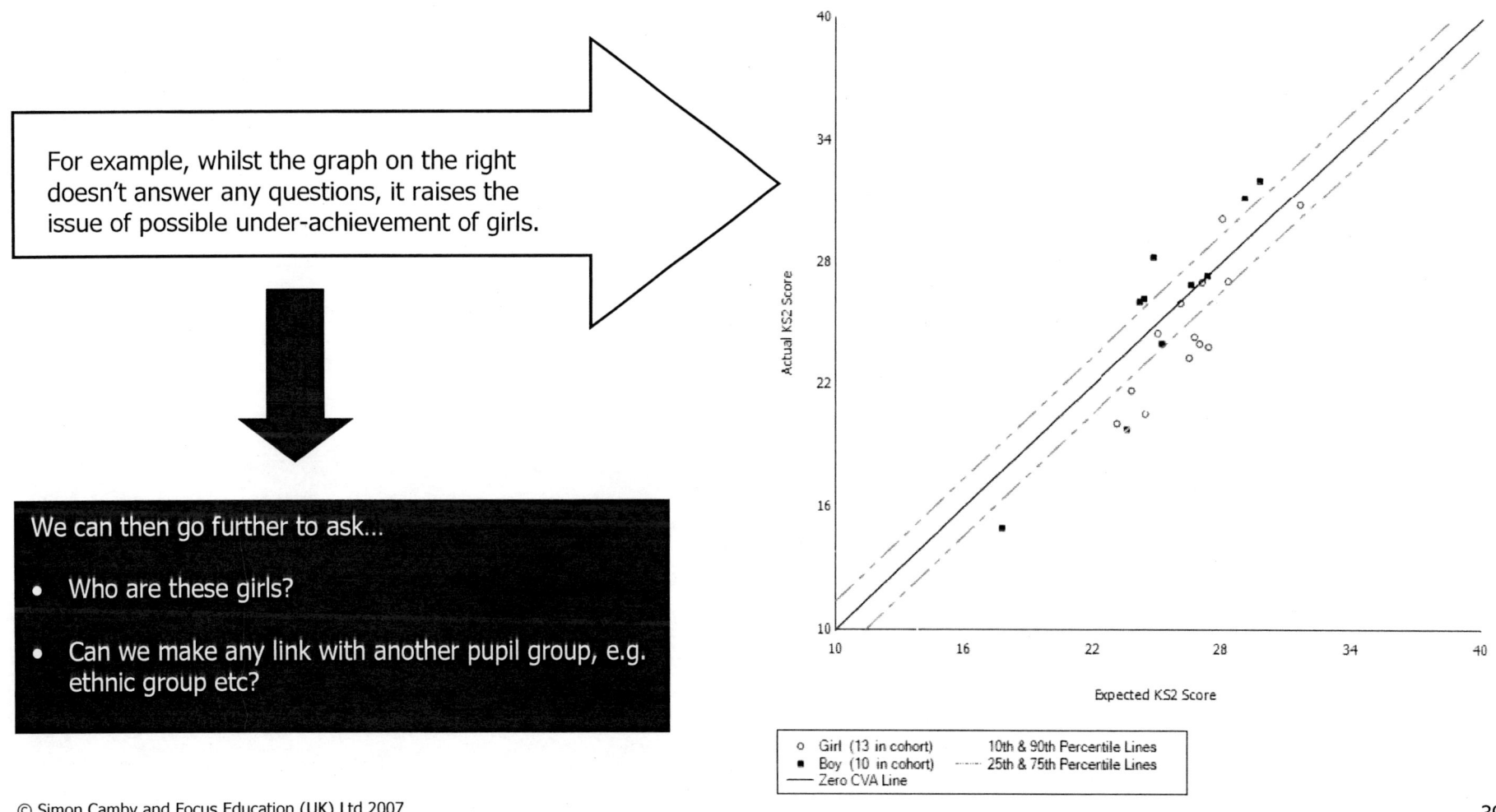

For example, whilst the graph on the right doesn't answer any questions, it raises the issue of possible under-achievement of girls.

We can then go further to ask...

- Who are these girls?

- Can we make any link with another pupil group, e.g. ethnic group etc?

Actual KS2 Score

Expected KS2 Score

o	Girl (10 in cohort)	10th & 90th Percentile Lines
■	Boy (10 in cohort)	25th & 75th Percentile Lines
—	Zero CVA Line	

SOME QUESTIONS TO CONSIDER IN RELATION TO CVA DATA

What does your CVA data tell you about the trend over time for the whole school?

What does your CVA data tell you about the trend over time for different subjects?

What is the difference between subjects? Does it stand out that you have a weaker area? Is there nay under-achievement?

Is there a difference of 1.5 points or more? (if so this is educationally important)

Do any specific pupil groups stand out? Are any sig+ or sig-

- Gender

- FSM/non-FSM

- EAL/non-EAL

- SEN/non-SEN/school action/school action plus/statements

- Ethnicity

- Other significant and/or vulnerable groups in your school

On the scatter-plot:

- Who are the children well below the line? Are they a specific group? How does this link with your own evaluations?

- Are there any clusters of children?, e.g. more able, less able, girls, boys etc

PULLING IT ALL TOGETHER

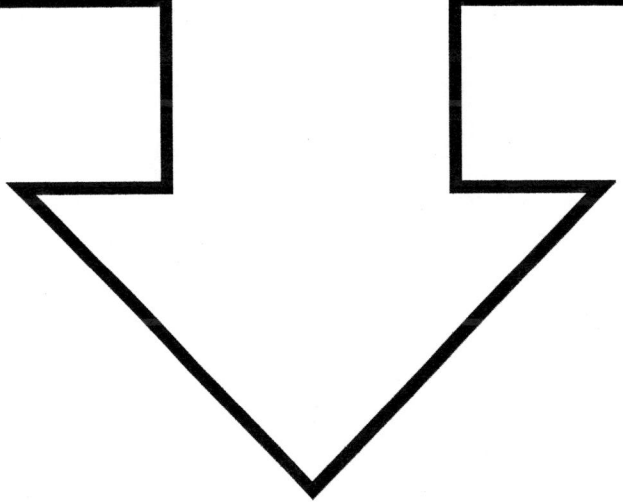

The following four pages outline descriptors and prompts for pulling all your analyses together. This should, in turn, write the standards and achievement section of your SEF (3b).

A. Extract from 'Evaluation schedule'. Ofsted guidance on grading standards and achievement

B. Grading chart from Ofsted Data Module – look for best fit pattern

C. Key stage one standards and achievement analysis – writing frame

D. Key stage two standards and achievement analysis – writing frame

E. Areas for improvement

A. OFSTED GUIDANCE ON GRADING STANDARDS AND ACHIEVEMENT

The following chart is an extract from the Ofsted Evaluation Schedule.
Use these descriptors, alongside the chart on the next page to make a judgement about standards and achievement.

Grade 1	Progress is al least good in nearly all respects and is exemplary in significant elements, as reflected in contextual value added measures.
Grade 2	Learners meet challenging targets and, in relation to their capacity and starting points, they achieve high standards. Most groups of learners, including those with learning difficulties and disabilities, make at least good progress and some may make very good progress, as reflected in contextual value added measures. Learners are gaining knowledge, skills and understanding at a good rate across all key stages. Most subjects are courses perform well, and some better than this, with nothing that is unsatisfactory.
Grade 3	Progress is inadequate in no major respect, and may be good in some respects, as reflected in contextual value added measures.
Grade 4	A significant number of learners do not meet targets that are adequately challenging. Contextual value added measures indicate slow progress. Considerably numbers of pupils underachieve, or particular groups of pupils underachieve significantly. The pace of learning is insufficient for learners to make satisfactory gains in knowledge, skills and understanding, especially in core subjects. Learners underachieve in one or more key stages. Performance in a number of subjects and courses is unsatisfactory. **Overall, the standards that learners achieve are not high enough when set against their capability and starting points.**

B. OFSTED GUIDANCE ON GRADING STANDARDS AND ACHIEVEMENT

Inspection teams use the following chart as a guide to grading standards and achievement.

GRADE	EDUCATIONAL IMPORTANCE	STATISTICAL SIGNIFICANCE	VARIATION
1	Exceptionally high standards: • KS1: 2 points above • KS2: 2.5 points above in all subjects Exceptionally high CVA in KS2: • 101.5 or greater	Sig+ on all measures if a large cohort. Not necessarily Sig+ for a small cohort as a long as results are consistent over time.	Consistently high performance over time, between groups and key stages.
2	No examples of exceptionally low or large negative for a key stage, subject or groups of pupils (even a small groups). No examples of large negatives for individuals without a convincing explanation.	No examples of Sig- for groups, no other important examples of Sig-.	No large variation that includes substantially below average performance. Note: children with learning difficulties and disabilities should not have notably lower CVA than others.
3	The only example of large negative being for a very small group or a few individuals.		
4	Exceptionally low standards: • KS1: 2 points below • KS2: 2.5 points below for any one core subject or any group of a significant size. Exceptionally low CVA in any one subject: • i.e. 98.5 or less	Sig- if a large cohort or group. Not necessarily Sig- for a small cohort if consistently low over time.	Consistently very low performance or varying with very low key stage, subject, group or significant number of individuals.

Extract from Ofsted Data Module: reference booklet

WORDS TO USE WHEN DESCRIBING STANDARDS AND PROGRESS	
Standards Grade 1: exceptionally and consistently high Grade 2: generally above average with none significantly below average Grade 3: broadly average Grade 4: exceptionally low	**Progress** Grade 1: outstanding Grade 2: good Grade 3: satisfactory Grade 4: inadequate

C. KEY STAGE ONE STANDARDS AND ACHIEVEMENT ANALYSIS

Evaluation of overall standards by the end of KS1	
Evaluation of subject specific issues based on KS1 standards	
Evaluation of pupil group issues based on KS1 standards	
What does the trend over time show?	
Based on what you know about attainment on entry and progress made, what do you know about achievement by the end of KS1?	
Is there any underachievement?	

D. KEY STAGE TWO STANDARDS AND ACHIEVEMENT ANALYSIS

Evaluation of overall standards by the end of KS2	
Evaluation of subject specific issues based on KS2 standards & CVA data	
Evaluation of pupil group issues based on KS2 standards & CVA data	
What does the trend over time show?	
Based on what you know about attainment on entry & standards by the end of KS1, what do you know about achievement by the end of KS2?	
Is there any underachievement?	
What about standards and achievement of current pupils? Are they on track to hit challenging targets?	

E. AREAS FOR IMPROVEMENT

Based on the evaluation from (C) above. What are the key priorities for improvement in KS1?	
Based on the evaluation from (D) above. What are the key priorities for improvement in KS2?	

WRITING FRAME FOR CRAFTING STANDARDS AND ACHIEVEMENT SECTION OF YOUR SEF

- Overall children achieve …

- By the end of key stage one…
  (Insert brief summary of standards. Pick out any highlights identifying any specific issues with subject and/or pupil groups)

- Current standards in key stage one…
  (What is your own in-school tracking telling you?)

- Based on end of foundation stage assessment this means that children make …
  (Insert judgement about progress and achievement)

- As a result we have identified that we need to…
  (Insert areas for improvement)

- By the end of key stage two…
  (Insert brief summary of standards. Pick out any highlights identifying any specific issues with subject and/or pupil groups)

- CVA data shows that…
  (State your argument if this doesn't show the whole picture. Point to your own data and other evidence to back this up)

- In relation to starting points, this means that overall achievement is…

- Based on our evaluation…
  (Insert your judgement about whether there is any under-achievement)

- Current tracking data shows…

- Achievement in non-core subjects…

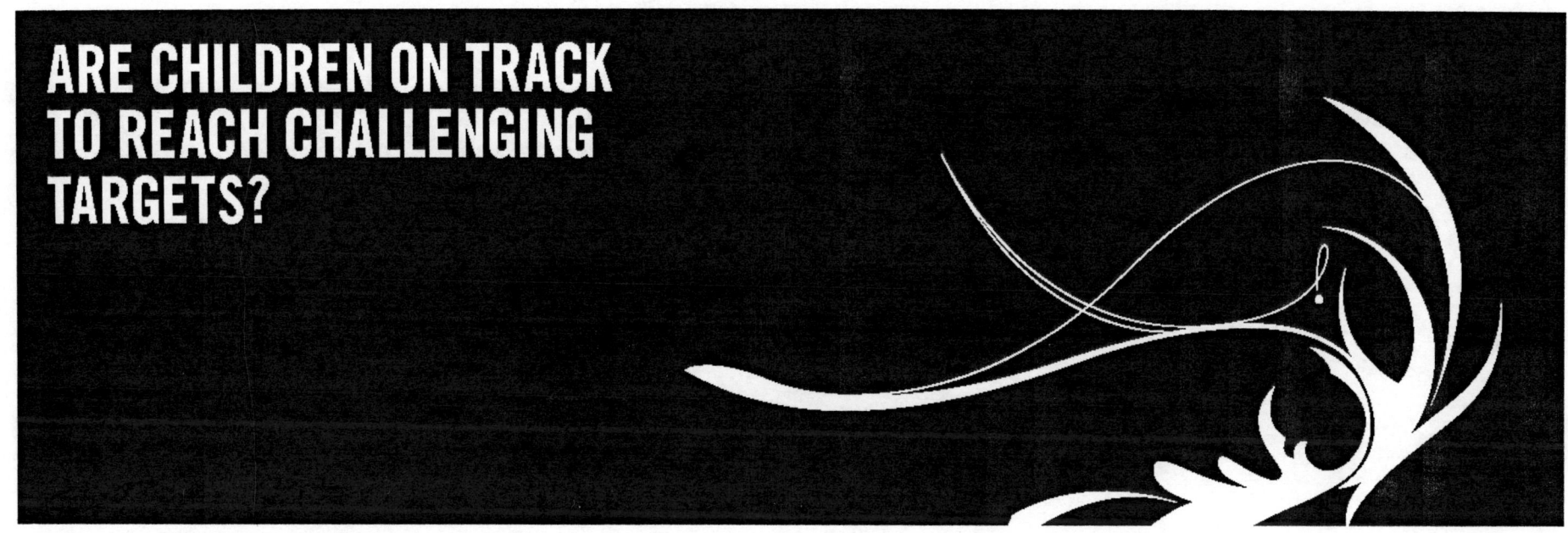

ARE CHILDREN ON TRACK TO REACH CHALLENGING TARGETS?

ARE CHILDREN IN TRACK TO REACH CHALLENGING TARGETS?

This is a key question which you need to be able to answer and should give an indication of in your self-evaluation. There are many ways you can prove this. Evidence to answer this question will come from (1) tracking data, (2) work scrutiny and (3) pupil discussion.

You can easily use Fischer Family Trust data to ensure that children are on track to reach challenging targets. You can also use the DfES Ready Reckoner (below) to give a broad indication of where a child's standards need to be in order to reach the CVA you aspire to as a school.

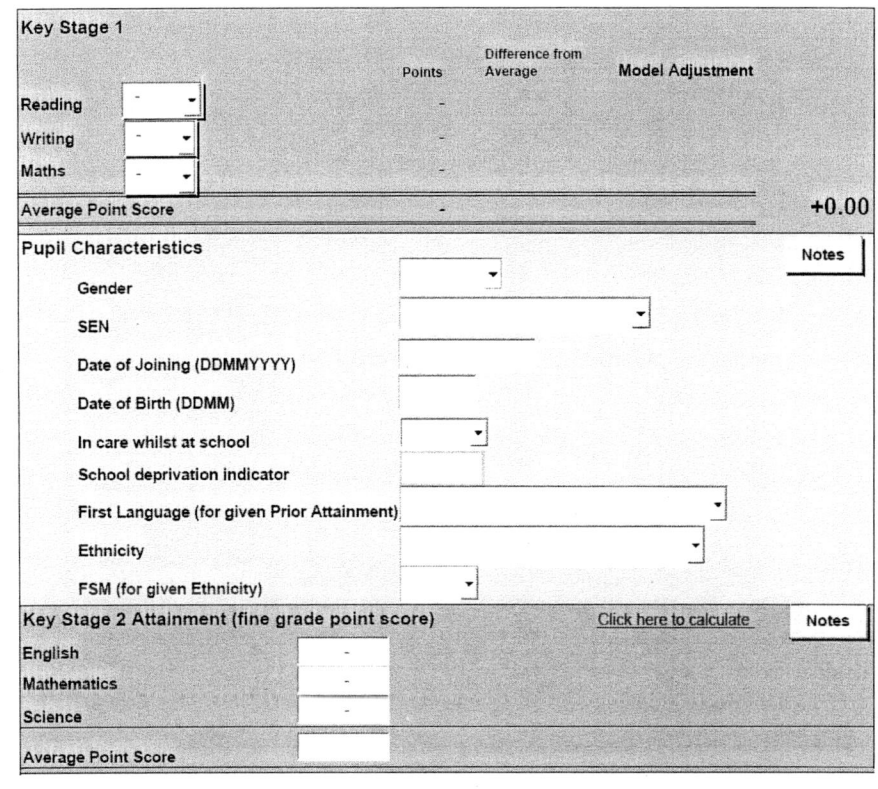

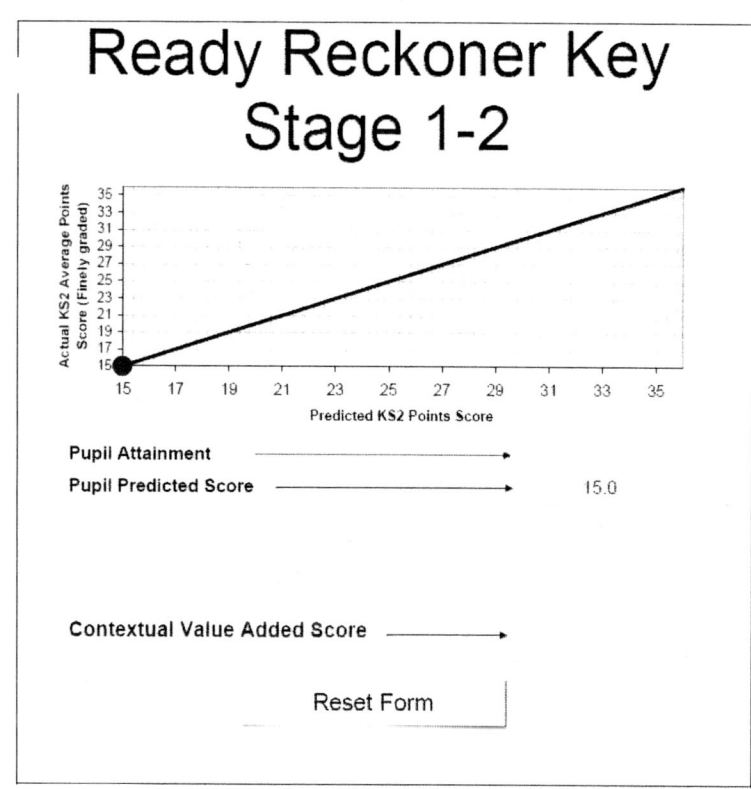

The Ready Reckoner is updated annually and is available to download from the DfES website. It is an interactive excel spreadsheet. Search: 'ready reckoner'

APPENDICES

- Cohort profile template (can be used to evaluate the outcomes for each cohort at the end of the academic year)

- RAISE on a side – simple chart to summarise all the key points from RAISE online

- How value added is calculated

- Glossary of terms used

TEMPLATE (i)　　　　COHORT ENTRY DATE ....

COHORT PROFILE

	NO OF CHILDREN	%
Number in cohort		
Boys		
Girls		

	NO OF CHILDREN	%
Autumn birthdays (Sep – Dec)		
Spring birthdays (Jan – Apr)		
Summer birthdays (May – Aug)		

	NO OF CHILDREN	%
In care		
SEN		
FSM		
EAL		

STAFF WORKING WITH THIS COHORT AND ANY RELEVANT NOTES

OTHER CONTEXTUAL NOTES ABOUT THIS COHORT

ETHNICITY	NO OF CHILDREN	%
White: British		
Irish		
Traveller or Irish Heritage		
Gypsy/Roma		
Any other white background		
Mixed: White and Black Caribbean		
White and Black African		
White and Asian		
Any other mixed background		
Asian or Asian British: Indian		
Pakistani		
Bangladeshi		
Any other Asian background		
Black or Black British: Caribbean		
African		
Any other Black background		
Chinese		
Any other ethnic background		

CHILDREN WHO JOINED MID YEAR

CHILDREN WHO LEFT MID YEAR

OVERALL STATEMENTS AND JUDGEMENTS	
Attainment statement	
Progress statement Make a statement about the progress made in relation to the starting points for the cohort.	
Achievement judgement Make a judgement about the achievement of the cohort taking account of where they started from, their context and capabilities.	
Are this cohort on track to reach end of key stage targets?	

TEMPLATE (iii)

EVALUATION ON ACHIEVEMENT OF SPECIFIC PUPIL GROUPS (WHERE RELEVANT)	
Boys/Girls	
SEN and more able children	
Autumn, Spring & Summer birthdays Term of entry (if relevant)	
Those who have attended pre-school and those who have not	For foundation stage.
Ethnicity	
Socio-economic backgrounds	
Any other pupil group relevant to the school/setting	

SO WHAT? (IMPLICATIONS)

Based on the evaluation and judgements made, what are the implications for this cohort as they move into the next school year?	Based on the evaluation and judgements made, what are the implications for provision in the current year?

RAISE ON-A-SIDE FOR STAFF AND GOVERNORS

	YEAR BEFORE	LAST YEAR	THIS YEAR
YEAR			
Overall CVA			
% rank			
English CVA			
% rank			
Maths CVA			
% rank			
Science CVA			
% rank			

KS1 standards	% L2+	% L3
Read		
Write		
Maths		
KS1 APS		
APS difference from national		

KS2 standards	% L4+	% L5
English		
Maths		
Science		
KS2 APS		
APS difference from national		

WHAT THE DATA SHOWS

WHAT WE NEED TO DO AS A RESULT

HOW IS VALUE ADDED AND CONTEXTUAL VALUE ADDED CALCULATED FOR YOUR SCHOOL?

It is important to understand how the data in your RAISE on-line report is arrived at.

There are different types of data:

Attainment data or Raw results	This is simply a record of outcomes based on test data at the end of key stages. Attainment data is expressed as an average point score (APS).
Relative attainment	
Contextual value added (CVA)	This is simply a record of outcomes based on test data at the end of key stages. Attainment data is expressed as an average point score (APS).

STEP 1:
The first calculation involves looking at every individual child's prior attainment at the end of key stage one.
Based on this prior attainment, a prediction is made as to where the child's attainment should be at the end of key stage two.
This prediction is made in line with the 'median line approach'. In other words it looks at all other children who attained the same prior attainment score and takes the score of the median child (note it is not the average).

STEP 2:
The second calculation involves working out the actual progress made by every individual child based on the different between their prior attainment and their actual attainment at the end of key stage two.

It is important to note that 'fine grades' are used to calculate progress at the end of key stage two. This means that the actual test marks are used rather than a whole level. So for example, a child who attains a high level 4 will gain more credit than a child who attains a low level 4.

The DfES Ready Reckoner (available on the DfES website) contains the exact details of average point score values for each mark awarded in the end of key stage tests.

HOW IS VALUE ADDED AND CONTEXTUAL VALUE ADDED CALCULATED FOR YOUR SCHOOL?

STEP 3:

This calculation involves taking account of the range of contextual factors which impact on pupil progress based on national data. In effect this calculation makes adjustments to predictions about progress. The following factors are used in the contextual value added calculation.

Gender	Allowing for an adjustment given the different rates of progress made by boys and girls.
Special Educational Needs	Allowing for an adjustment for those who are school action, school action plus or who are statemented.
Ethnicity	Allowing for an adjustment for each of the 19 ethnic groups recorded in PLASC.
Eligibility for Free School Meals	Allowing for an adjustment for pupils eligible for free school meals. The size of the adjustment depends on the pupil's ethnic group, because evidence suggests that the size of the FSM effect varies between different ethnic groups.
First Language	Allowing for an adjustment for the effect of pupils whose first language is other than English. The size of the adjustment depends on the pupil's prior attainment. This is because the effect of this factor tends to taper, with the greatest effect for pupils starting below expected levels and lesser effects for pupils already working at higher levels.
Mobility	Allowing for pupils who have moved between schools at non-standard transfer times.
Age	Allowing for pupils age based on date of birth.
In Care	Allowing for pupils who are 'in care' whilst at school.
IDACI (Income Deprivation Affecting Children Index)	This is a measure of deprivation based on pupil postcode focusing on the proportion of children under the age of 16 in an area living in low income homes. The indicator ranges from 0.00 to 1.00 with 0.14 being around average (2005 data).

STEP 4:

The final contextual value added outcome then takes account of the difference (positive or negative) between their predicted and actual attainment.

GLOSSARY OF TERMS

APS
Average Point Score. This is the average of the points achieved by pupils in a cohort in national tests.

A/T
Absent or working at the level of the tests but unable to access them. The percentage of eligible pupils who were absent at the time of the test or unable to access it. Each school's results are based on the achievements of all its eligible pupils, including any pupils absent or unable to access the test. The school's results may have been affected by these pupils, because they are included in the calculations but did not achieve a result. The higher the percentage shown, the more the school's results may have been affected by pupils with no results.

ATTAINMENT
Results that are not measured in terms of progress against previous achievement.

CONTEXT
The demographic profile of a school.

CONVERSION
A report that shows what proportion of pupils at the various levels of attainment at the previous key stage attain a given level in a later key stage.

COVERAGE INDICATOR
It shows the percentage of pupils eligible for KS2 assessment that are included in the value added calculation and gives some indication of schools where the value added measure may be unrepresentative.

CVA
Contextual Value Added. A school performance measure that takes account of contextual factors to determine whether pupils in a school have made more or less progress when compared to the national average.

ELIGIBLE PUPIL
Number of pupils eligible for Key Stage 2 assessment in the 2005/2006 school year

All pupils, including those with SEN, are eligible for assessment under the National Curriculum when they reach the end of Key Stage 2. Most will be aged 11 by the end of the school year, but some will be older or younger. This number includes all eligible pupils on the school roll at the time of the tests in May, regardless of whether or not they sat the tests (some pupils may have been absent or working at the level of the tests but unable to access them).

L4+
The percentage of eligible pupils achieving Level 4 or above in the test. Level 4 is the level expected of most 11 year olds. This percentage is based on all eligible pupils, including those who were absent at the time of the test or working at the level of the tests but unable to access them and, therefore, did not achieve a result.

L5+
The percentage of eligible pupils achieving Level 5 in the test. Level 5 means pupils are achieving beyond the expected level. This percentage is based on all eligible pupils, including those who were absent at the time of the test or working at the level of the tests but unable to access them and, therefore, did not achieve a result.

GLOSSARY OF TERMS

MOBILITY

The mobility column shows the percentage of pupils eligible for KS2 assessment who were in the school for the whole of their KS2 education (Year 3 - Year 6 inclusive).

The mobility indicator is based on pupils' dates of entry to the school. Where schools have recently merged or opened, pupils' dates of entry are set to the school's date of opening or later. In these cases, the mobility indicator may appear to be low.

A relatively low mobility percentage means that a high proportion of the pupils eligible for the KS2 tests were not in the school for the whole of their KS2 education.

FULL REPORT

A downloadable document containing the main analyses for a school in a similar form to the previous PANDA.

STANDARDS

Ofsted provide the following description:

Standards are compared with those reached by pupils nationally.

[also see attainment]

THRESHOLD

A report showing what proportion of a cohort achieves a certain level or result at the end of a key stage.

VA

Value Added. This is a school performance measure that measures pupils' progress by using only previous attainment as a benchmark. No contextual information is used in this calculation.